Contents

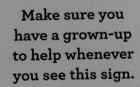

Make sure you have a grown-up to help whenever you see this sign.

!

What a Waste!

People produce loads of rubbish. Throughout the world, we create a billion tonnes of it each year. Even cavemen produced it. Their caves soon filled with old bones, wood and other waste, so eventually they had to move to a new cave. Today, we create more rubbish than ever before. But many of the things we think of as rubbish are not waste at all. They are made from valuable materials taken from the environment (called raw materials) that could be used again.

Wasted Cars

In the United States, over 12 million cars are scrapped each year. Most of a car's parts can be recycled, but there's still a lot of waste leftover.

Instead of being thrown away, much of the rubbish seen here could be reused, or recycled, to make new things. This would mean taking fewer raw materials from our environment.

Food waste

Glass bottles and jars

Plastic

These are just some of the many things we think of as waste. But the real waste is throwing away so many valuable materials, such as paper, glass, wood and metals. Even kitchen waste can be reused.

D ... self

... d

First published 2020 by Kingfisher
an imprint of Macmillan Children's Books
The Smithson, 6 Briset Street,
London, EC1M 5NR
Associated companies
throughout the world
www.panmacmillan.com

Copyright © Macmillan Publishers
International Ltd 1999, 2020

Designed by: Tall Tree
Illustrated by: Diego Vaisberg/
Advocate Art

Material previously published in
Young Discoverers Rubbish and Recycling (1999)

ISBN: 978-0-7534-4552-5

9 8 7 6 5 4 3 2 1
1TR/0420/WKT/128MA

A CIP catalogue record for this book is
available from the British Library.

Printed in China

DISCOVER IT YOURSELF!

Much of the rubbish we throw out comes from packaging (the materials used to wrap food and other goods we buy from shops). Find out how much packaging your family uses in one week and see whether any of it can be recycled.

Next time you or a member of your family goes shopping, count the number of layers of wrapping on some of the items. Packaging holds the goods together and makes them look attractive. But often you will find there are lots of unnecessary layers.

Toy car

Cake

Box of chocolates

Paper and card

Tin cans

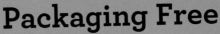

Packaging Free

Supermarkets and shops are trying to reduce the amount of packaging and plastic used. Shoppers are encouraged to bring their own bags and lots of produce comes packaging free.

5

Where Does It Go?

Each week, our rubbish is put out in rubbish bins to be taken away. Much of it ends up being buried in a landfill. This is a big hole in the ground, such as a disused quarry or sand pit. But burying rubbish takes up a lot of space and spoils the countryside. Sometimes the rubbish is taken to an incinerator where it is burnt. The heat may be used to make electricity for local homes. But burning it produces harmful fumes that pollute the air.

Energy from Waste

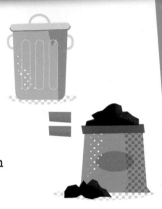

Burning rubbish to make electricity is a useful way of getting rid of waste. One bin of rubbish can generate as much electricity as a bag of coal.

Not all rubbish is wasted. Rotting rubbish gives off a gas called methane, which can be burnt to make electricity. Kitchen and garden waste can be made into compost and sprayed on fields. Many materials can be recycled into new products.

Burnt in an incinerator

Methane gas used to make electricity

Buried in landfill

Used as compost

Recycled to make new goods

Rubbish put in a landfill is squashed down before more rubbish is placed on top. Eventually, the hole is filled. Then it can be covered with soil and turned into a park or a sports field.

Recycling is a good way to help our planet. It saves materials, energy and land that might otherwise be used as landfill. It also reduces pollution.

DISCOVER IT YOURSELF!

Collect unwanted objects from your home and donate them to a charity.

Charities collect a wide range of items that might otherwise get thrown away. Find out what your local charity store collects and have a charity drive at home. Instead of being burnt, your waste could end up helping someone.

Nature's Recycling

Have you noticed that you never see huge piles of dead trees and animals in woodlands? This is because natural materials quickly decompose (break down) and are recycled. These materials are said to be biodegradable. Nature is very good at recycling, so nothing goes to waste. Insects, earthworms, fungi and microscopic bacteria are important because their job is to break down materials. They are called decomposers.

Eye-Spy

Look out for waste that is biodegradable. Apple cores, dead leaves, old clothes, cardboard boxes and newspapers will all eventually rot or get eaten.

Acorn

Young oak tree

Squirrel eating acorns

Dead squirrel

Minibeasts

Fungi

There is no waste in nature. Fallen leaves and dead animals are soon eaten by insects or rotted by fungi. This releases food substances called nutrients into the soil, which are absorbed by young trees. Animals feed on the trees. When they die, the cycle begins again.

DISCOVER IT YOURSELF!

Catch some insect decomposers using this simple method.

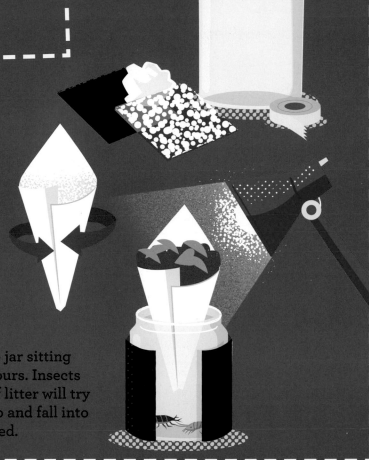

1. Cut a piece of paper about 30 centimetres x 20 centimetres (12 inches × 8 inches). Roll it up to make a funnel shape and tape it together. The hole at the bottom should be about 1 centimetre (½ centimetre) across.

2. Put some damp tissue in the bottom of a glass jar and wrap the jar with a piece of black paper. Put your funnel in the jar.

3. Collect leaf litter from under some trees. (Leaf litter is a damp mixture of rotten leaves and soil.)

4. Fill your funnel with leaf litter and leave the jar sitting under a strong light from a table lamp for two hours. Insects prefer dark damp places, so the ones in your leaf litter will try to crawl away from the heat and light of the lamp and fall into the jar. Release the insects when you have finished.

More Things to Try

Build a home for your decomposers by turning a large jar on its side. Make breathing holes in a lid and put some soil, rotten wood and leaf litter inside, along with your insects. Add plenty of food such as apple or potato peels and keep the soil damp. Then cover the jar with a dark cloth. Return the creatures to their natural habitat after a few days.

Worms at Work

Worms are good recyclers. They feed on dead and rotting matter, such as leaves, that they find on the ground. This helps to break down the matter so it can be reused by plants.

Rubbish That Won't Rot

If you left a plastic bag, a glass bottle or an aluminium can outside, it would stay there unchanged for hundreds of years. This is because plastic, glass and some metals are non-biodegradable – they will never rot. Of course, it is important for some materials to be non-biodegradable. Building materials, glass and many plastics must stay intact to do their job properly. But when no longer needed, these materials are difficult to dispose of.

Much of the rubbish we throw away each week will never rot. We have to keep creating new landfill sites to take it all. One day, our planet could become one big rubbish tip!

DISCOVER IT YOURSELF!

Do a litter survey to find out how much litter there is on your road, around your school and in your local park.

Draw a chart like the one shown here. Mark on your chart how much litter you find in each place and what kind of litter it is. Clear the litter up as you go by putting it in a rubbish bag. Be sure to wear gloves when you touch litter.

	Road	Park	Garden
Glass	++++ ++	++++	
Paper	++++	++++ ++	++
Plastic		++	++++	+
Metal	+++	++++	

? How Can We Help?

- Never drop litter. Rubbish that is made of plastics, Styrofoam, metals and glass will not rot away.

- Do a litter survey like the one here, and organize a "litter blitz" to clear it all up.

Eye-Spy

Because most litter does not rot, it will stay in our environment for many years unless it is cleaned up. Check the dates on litter, such as crisp bags, to see how old it is.

Litter gets everywhere, from our roads to our beaches, and it is not a pretty sight. People who drop non-biodegradable waste outdoors are spoiling the environment for everyone else.

DISCOVER IT YOURSELF!
Find out which rubbish is biodegradable and which is not by doing this simple test.

1. Collect some plastic containers and fill them with damp soil.

2. Find several bits of man-made rubbish and several bits of natural rubbish. Bury each object in a pot and identify it with a label. Leave the pots somewhere cool and damp for a couple of weeks, then dig up the objects to see if they have rotted or changed at all.

 ## ? How It Works

The natural rubbish will have started to decompose or may have rotted away altogether because it is biodegradable. The man-made rubbish does not decompose and will not have changed at all. Luckily, we can recycle much of our non-biodegradable rubbish so that it can be used again.

Waste Not, Want Not

It is very wasteful to throw things away if they can be reused or recycled. Raw materials have to be taken from the environment to make new things, which uses energy and causes pollution. So the more we throw away, the more the environment will be harmed. The number of materials we can recycle is increasing all the time. Once, only glass and metal were recyclable. Today, we can also recycle paper, cardboard, cloth, batteries, plastics and much more.

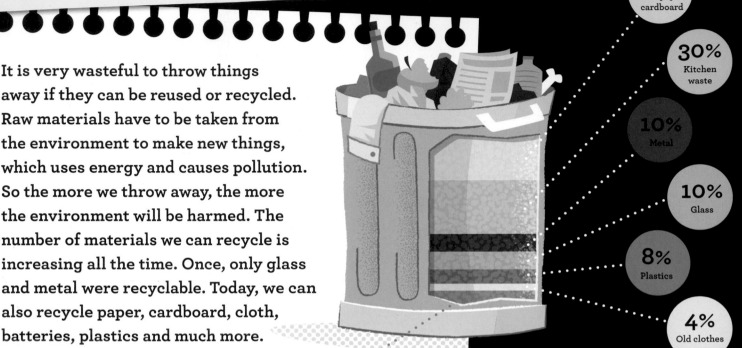

30% Wastepaper + cardboard

30% Kitchen waste

10% Metal

10% Glass

8% Plastics

4% Old clothes

8% Other materials, including dust

This diagram shows the different amounts of waste that get thrown out in our rubbish each week. If we were more careful, we could recycle three-fourths of our household waste.

Christmas Recycling

Instead of throwing your old Christmas tree in the rubbish, take it to a recycling centre where you may be able to get it chipped into tiny pieces for reuse as garden compost.

DISCOVER IT YOURSELF!

Find out how much rubbish your family produces in a week and sort it into bags ready for recycling.

1. Find seven plastic bags and tape a piece of scrap paper onto each one so you can write down what it contains. You will need a bag for each of the following: metal, paper, cardboard, plastics, glass, old clothes or fabrics and food scraps.

2. Sort your rubbish into the different bags and see how much you collect in a week. How does your rubbish compare with the amounts shown in the diagram opposite? Remember to wear gloves and wash your hands after handling rubbish.

? How Can We Help?

We should all try to cut down on the amount of rubbish we produce. The best way to do so it remember the three Rs:

Reduce
Reuse
Recycle

We can reduce waste by buying less in the first place, reusing items, such as plastic bags and glass jars, instead of throwing them away and recycling our rubbish so that materials are not wasted.

Eye-Spy

Next time you empty a bottle or drinks can, finish a comic book, or tear a T-shirt, think whether the leftovers can be recycled or donated to charity.

Gardens and Garages

A lot of recycling can be done at home. For example, biodegradable kitchen and garden waste, such as food scraps and grass cuttings, can be put on a compost heap. The waste quickly rots down to form a compost, which makes a good fertilizer (food) for garden plants. Your garage may be full of old junk that usually ends up in the local rubbish tip. Some of it might find a new life as a flower container or a rain barrel.

Fallen leaves can be recycled by digging them into the soil. As they rot, the leaves form a substance called humus, which makes a good plant food.

DISCOVER IT YOURSELF!

Build a compost heap or "worm factory" for your kitchen waste, so you can recycle food scraps into a rich compost that will help your plants to grow.

1. Ask an adult to drill two lines of holes around the bottom of an old rubbish bin as shown here. This will allow any liquid to drain out of your can.

- Never pour oil down the drain – it causes water pollution.
- Put garden waste on a compost heap or take it to a recycling centre.
- Use old pieces of wood to make bird feeders or nesting boxes.

Old tyres and broken wheelbarrows can be recycled to make unusual flower containers. Pots are often made of recycled materials. Some garages take old tyres for recycling. Or you can take them to a recycling centre, along with any broken tools.

2. Put a layer of gravel or rocks, about 18 cm (7 inches) deep, in the bottom of your bin. Follow this with a layer of sand about 8 cm (3 inches) deep. The sand and rocks will allow water to drain through your bin while still keeping the contents damp.

3. Add a layer of wooden slats to stop the compost mixing with the sand. Put about 15 cm (6 inches) of potting compost on top.

4. Buy some earthworms from a fishing shop and lay them in the compost. Feed them regularly with kitchen waste, such as vegetable peels, crushed eggshells and cheese rinds. Do not feed them meat or fruit.

5. Leave the lid on your worm factory to keep it warm and damp. The compost will be ready to use on your garden after two to three months.

6. Pick out the worms before you put the compost on your garden. Return them to their worm factory so they can get back to work!

Down the Drain

Every day, we each use litres of water to clean ourselves and to flush the toilet. We also use water for cooking, and in dishwashers and washing machines, as well as for washing the car. Once we have finished with the water, it disappears down the drain. But that is not the last we see of it. It is then cleaned and recycled so we can use it again. There always seems to be plenty of fresh water. But sometimes, if there has been a drought, there is hardly enough to go around. So we must all try to reduce the amount of water we use.

How Many Times?

In many large cities, water from the tap has been recycled as many as 20 times! But it is still perfectly safe to drink.

DISCOVER IT YOURSELF!

Do a water survey to see how much water is used at home by your family in a day.

	How often?
Water filter	IIII
Cooking	ЖІ
Washing car	I
Laundry	III
Dishwasher	II
Toilet	ЖІІ
Shower/Bath	IIII
Watering plants	II
Sprinkler	I

Draw a chart like the one here, listing all the things that use up water in your home, such as flushing the toilet or having a bath. Mark it on your chart each time someone uses water. How is water used most often? Could you think of ways to use less water?

THE WATER CYCLE

Your home

Treatment plant

Clean water pumped into rivers

Reservoir supplies homes

Water evaporates

Dirty water from your home goes to a treatment plant to be cleaned. Then it is poured into rivers and carried to the sea. Some water evaporates (turns into a gas) and forms clouds. When rainwater falls, it fills up the reservoirs that supply us with water.

DISCOVER IT YOURSELF!

See how quickly water evaporates.

Measure out ¼ cup of water into each of three different containers: a saucer, a glass and a bottle. Leave them on a sunny windowsill for a day.

From which container has the most water disappeared?

? How It Works

The water evaporates fastest from the saucer because it has a large surface area open to the air. It takes longest to evaporate from the bottle because there is little surface area open to the air and only a small hole to escape through.

DISCOVER IT YOURSELF!

Water is cleaned at a treatment plant by filtering it through soil, sand and gravel to remove all the dirt. Try making your own water filter.

1. Line a funnel with a coffee filter paper and place it into a glass jar. Put a layer of fine sand, about 4 centimetres (1½ inches) deep, in the bottom of the lining paper.

2. Mix a handful of soil with some water. Pour the dirty water into the funnel and see how well the sand filters out the soil. Does the water come out clean?

? How It Works

As the water trickles through the sand, pieces of dirt are trapped by the sand particles and the water is cleaned.

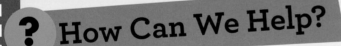

? How Can We Help?

Save water – it is too precious to waste.
- Turn off taps so they don't drip.
- Take a shower instead of a bath – you will save 30–46 litres (7–12 gallons) every time.
- Put a brick in the tank so less water is wasted when you flush the toilet.

Water containing sewage (human waste) is treated at a sewage plant (shown right). The solids are removed, then the liquid part is trickled through filter beds where bacteria break down any germs.

Eye-Spy

A special symbol is used to show that something has been made from recycled paper. How many things can you spot in your house that have this symbol on them?

Paper is a very useful material. It is used to make books, newspapers, paper money, writing paper, magazines and much more. Most of it is made from conifer trees. The wood is chipped into tiny pieces and mixed with water and chemicals to produce a pulp. Then it is drained, squeezed and dried to form a huge roll of paper. Paper and cardboard are easily recycled. The old paper is chopped up and put back into the paper-making process at the pulping stage.

This diagram shows the different stages in making paper, from chipping, pulping and refining to rolling and drying.

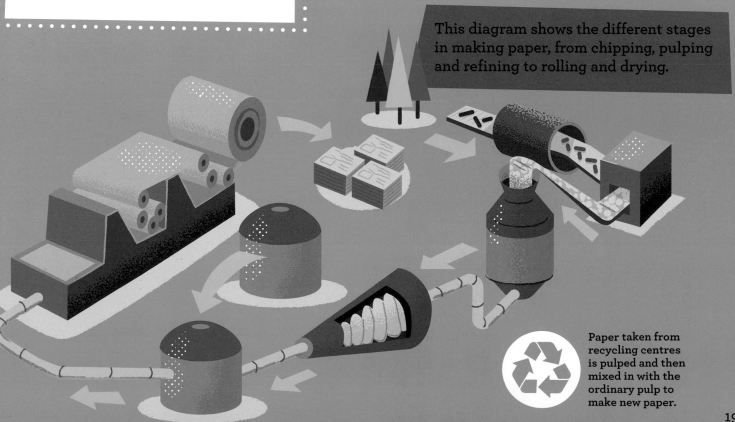

Paper taken from recycling centres is pulped and then mixed in with the ordinary pulp to make new paper.

19

Why Recycle It?

Recycling paper means less rubbish needs to be buried in landfills. Making new paper from old also saves on chemicals, energy and water. But it does not really save trees because most paper is made from conifers that are grown specially for this purpose.

The trees used for making paper come from conifer plantations. As trees are cut down, new trees are planted in their place, so there is a constant supply of wood. Unfortunately, the plantations replace natural habitats, such as forests, that are rich in wildlife. By recycling paper we are helping to save wildlife.

? How Can We Help?

If we did not recycle our paper, we would need to cut down five million trees every day!

- Recycle newspapers and cardboard.
- Reuse old envelopes by putting a sticky label over the old address.
- Whenever possible, draw or write on both sides of your paper so you don't waste any.
- Collect scrap paper and staple it together to make a phone message pad.

How Much Paper?

On average, a person in the United States uses 310 kilograms (680 pounds) of paper every year, almost twice as much as someone in England and 100 times more than in India.

| U.S.A. 310 kg (683 lb) | England 163 kg (359 lb) | India 3 kg (6 lb) |

DISCOVER IT YOURSELF!

Make some recycled paper. You will need an adult to help you.

1. Tear up several newspapers into thin strips and leave them to soak in a bucket of water overnight.

2. Ask an adult to boil the mixture in an old pan for 10 minutes until the paper dissolves into a mushy stew. Leave it to cool. Then pour the mixture into a wide, flat plastic bowl.

3. Ask the adult to help you make a frame that will fit into your bowl. You will need to cut four lengths of wood and nail them together at the corners.

4. Cut a piece of fine plastic mesh slightly bigger than your frame. You can buy the mesh from a garden centre. Choose a mesh with holes less than 0.5 centimetres (¼ inch) across. Tack or staple the mesh onto the frame.

5. Starting with the frame held upright, scoop it into the bucket and under the pulp that is floating on the surface of the water. Then lift the frame out flat so that there is an even layer of pulp all over it.

6. When the water has drained away, turn the pulp out onto a piece of felt or an old blanket. Add two more layers of pulp.

7. Place another piece of felt or blanket on top, then a hard board. Step on the board to squeeze out all the water, then remove the top blanket and board and leave the paper to dry.

Banks for Bottles

Glass has been used for thousands of years. It is made by heating sand, soda and limestone together at very high temperatures so that they melt and form a liquid. As the liquid cools, it turns into glass. Glass is easy to recycle. The old glass is cleaned and broken up, then it is melted and moulded into shape just like new glass. Recycling means taking fewer raw materials from the ground. It also helps to save energy.

Buying milk and orange juice in returnable glass bottles saves energy and raw materials because the bottles can be reused up to 11 times. A carton can be used only once.

Glass from a bottle bank is cleaned and broken up into small pieces, called cullet. The cullet is melted down in a furnace and the liquid glass is then poured into a mould and left to cool. The bottles are filled and capped, ready for the supermarket shelves.

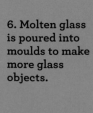

1. Bottles put into a bottle bank.

2. Glass bottles are taken to the recycling centre.

3. Bottles are sorted.

4. Glass bottles are crushed into small pieces.

5. Glass pieces are put in a furnace and melted.

6. Molten glass is poured into moulds to make more glass objects.

Glass Recycling

A mountain of glass lies waiting to be recycled. Glass is sorted into different colours before it is processed. Clear glass is the most useful because it can be made into all kinds of bottles and jars, but green glass has fewer uses— it is mostly made into wine bottles.

DISCOVER IT YOURSELF!

Instead of recycling it, reuse a glass bottle to make this pretty table decoration.

1. Buy a block of florists' foam from a flower shop and cut off a small piece about 7.5 centimetres (3 inches) square and 4 centimetres (1½ inches) deep.

2. Cut a hole in the middle big enough to fit over the neck of the bottle. Soak the foam in water, then put it over the neck. Now place a candle in the bottle and fill the foam with pretty flowers and ivy. (Do not light the candle without an adult present or leave the candle unattended.)

? How Can We Help?

- Take unwanted glass to a bottle bank to be recycled.

- Buy milk, orange juice and fizzy drinks in reusable glass bottles rather than cartons and plastic bottles whenever possible.

- Reuse bottles and jars as containers or vases (see below for ideas).

Not all recycled glass is used to make new bottles and jars. Some is used to make bathroom tiles, bricks, reflective road signs and fibreglass boats and kayaks.

DISCOVER IT YOURSELF!

Use some of your old glass bottles to make a bottle orchestra.

Collect some empty bottles and jars of all shapes and sizes and wash them out. Fill them with different amounts of water to give a range of notes, then "play" them by tapping them with a metal spoon. See if you can play any tunes you know.

More Things to Try

Reuse glass bottles and jars by turning them into containers for pens and pencils, flowers, marbles and much more. Paint them with crazy designs or glue paper scraps, or decorate them with stickers.

24

Cans Count

What to Recycle?

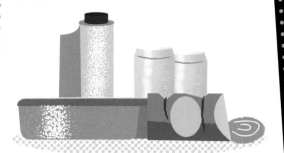

All sorts of metal items can be recycled, including steel and aluminium food and drinks cans, bottle tops and aluminium foil and frozen food trays.

Metal food cans have been used for about 200 years. Cans are ideal for storing food and drink for long periods. We use millions of them every day. The metal used in cans is valuable, so recycling is very important. There is no limit to the number of times the metal can be recycled. Steel made from old cans uses just one-fourth of the energy that would be needed to make steel from raw materials. Recycling also means digging up fewer raw materials, creating less rubbish and filling up fewer landfills.

Everything made of steel contains some steel that has been recycled. The steel in a can of beans could end up in a bridge, a car, a knife or just a simple paper clip.

Cans in Space

Every year, billions of cans are used in the United States alone. If they were lined up end to end, they would stretch to the Moon and back many times!

Aluminium and Steel Cans

The first cans were made from iron coated with a thin layer of tin, which is why we still call them tin cans. Nowadays, cans are made from steel or aluminium. Drinks cans have to be light, so they are made from a very thin sheet of metal. Food cans have to be thicker and stronger so they can protect their contents.

Eye-Spy

Most drinks cans now have a symbol or logo on their side, reminding you to recycle them. Here are some of the symbols to look out for.

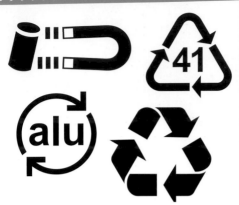

Inside a recycling plant, special machines are used to squash aluminium cans into bales. The cans are then melted down and rolled out to form sheet aluminium, ready to be used again.

DISCOVER IT YOURSELF!

Do this simple test to see if a can is made of steel or aluminium.

Steel is magnetic – that is, it is attracted to magnets – and aluminium is not. So hold the can up to a magnet and see if it sticks. If it does, it is made of steel. If it does not, it is made of aluminium.

Check other metal objects to see if they are magnetic, such as needles, keys, pencil sharpeners, foil and bottle tops. If they are, they are made of steel or iron.

Saving Energy

The amount of energy needed to make one aluminium can from raw materials is the same as that required to make 20 cans from recycled aluminium.

- Take empty food and drinks cans to your local recycling centre.
- Encourage your school to get a can bank so you can all collect cans for recycling.
- Don't forget that foil, bottle tops and frozen food trays can be recycled too!

DISCOVER IT YOURSELF!

Use a couple of empty food cans and a length of string to make your own "mobile phone".

1. Ask an adult to file down any sharp edges on the cans. Then wash them out.

2. With an adult's help, make a hole in each can, in the centre of the base, using a hammer and nail.

3. Cut a piece of string 20 metres (65 feet) long. Feed each end through the hole in the base of each can. Tie the ends off with a knot on the inside.

4. Ask a friend to hold a can up to his or her ear and stand as far away from you as possible. Keeping the string pulled tight, speak into your can and see if your friend can hear you.

? How It Works

Your voice makes the can vibrate as you speak into it. The vibrations are carried along the string to the other can, which also vibrates, reproducing the sound of your voice so your friend can hear you speaking.

Recycling Plastics

Plastic is a very useful material that is cheap and easy to make. This is why we use so much of it. In the United States, two and a half million plastic bottles are used every hour! Most plastic is non-biodegradable, which makes it difficult to get rid of. The best way is to recycle it and make something new with it. Oil is used to make many plastics, so recycling also saves oil.

Record discs are made from plastic. There are millions of unwanted records in the world now being collected and made into credit cards!

A surprising range of objects can be made using recycled plastic, from bags and bottles to boots, pots and pipes.

Eye-Spy

These logos are used on plastic packaging to show that it can be recycled. A different number is used for each type of plastic. Can you find these logos on containers in your home?

 PETE
HDPE
V
LDPE

 PP
PS
OTHER

DISCOVER IT YOURSELF!

Reuse a plastic bottle to make an unusual plant holder. Ask an adult to help you with the cutting.

!

1. Find an empty 2 litres (64 ounces) plastic drinks bottle and peel off the label. Using a felt-tip pen, draw two rings around the bottle, one 7 centimetres (3 inches) from the bottom, the other 13 centimetres (5 inches) from the top.

2. Draw two lines, 2 centimetres (³/₄ inch) apart, down the length of the bottle between the two rings. Draw three more sets of lines, evenly spacing them around the bottle. Ask an adult to cut out the large rectangles between your lines.

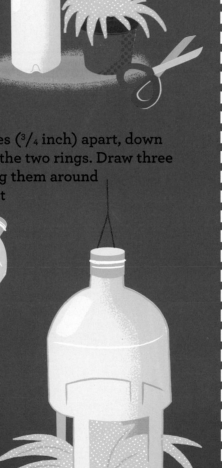

3. Make two holes in the top of the bottle and thread string through to hang up your container. Finally, put a small plant inside.

Fast Food

Styrofoam fast-food containers trap the heat so that the food does not get cold. It is difficult to recycle, so most ends up in landfill.

Plastics for recycling are first sorted into the different types. Then they are washed and shredded into tiny pieces, or chips, before being melted down and turned into something new.

? How Can We Help?

- Take plastic bottles and other packaging to your local recycling centre.
- Take an old plastic bag with you when you go shopping so you don't need to be given a new one.
- Reuse plastic ice cream tubs as sandwich or freezer boxes.
- Use yoghurt containers to mix paint or glue in.

Recycle Your Rags

Old clothes and rags should never be thrown away. Just like glass and paper, rags can be recycled. Some fabrics are ripped up to make a substance called "shoddy". This is used to make furniture fabrics, blankets, carpets and even new clothes. Other fabrics are turned into stuffing for mattresses, and some are used as wiping cloths for machinery.

Sent to people in poor countries

Burnt as rubbish

Recycled as blankets, furnishing fabrics, carpets and clothes

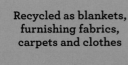

Old wool clothes are used to make shoddy. First they have to be sorted into colours – sometimes as many as 50 different ones!

Some old clothes are collected by charities and are resold or sent to poorer countries. A few clothes are burnt as rubbish. But the rest can be recycled.

Recycled as wiping cloths for factory machinery

DISCOVER IT YOURSELF!

Turn an old sock into a fun puppy puppet. You could even make lots of different animals and put on your own puppet show.

1. Find an old sock and sew up any holes.

2. Using a felt-tip pen, draw two ears, two eyes, a nose and a tongue onto brightly coloured felt or cotton fabric. Copy the shapes given here, making them as big as you like. Or draw different shapes and make a mouse, a cat or some other animal.

3. Now glue or sew all the different shapes onto your sock.

4. To use your puppet, put your hand inside the sock so that the heel sits over your knuckles. Push the toe in on itself to form the mouth. Then tap your fingers and thumb together to make your puppet "talk".

? How Can We Help?

- Take good quality old clothes to car-boot sales or charity shops.

- Take damaged old clothes, blankets and material to a clothes bank. Your local government office should be able to tell you where your nearest one is.

- Tear up old towels or sheets and use them as polishers or dusters.

Index